CASUAL CONVERSATION

A BLESSING THE BOATS SELECTION

CASUAL CONVERSATION

POEMS BY

Renia White

FOREWORD BY ARACELIS GIRMAY
BLESSING THE BOATS SELECTION EDITOR–AT–LARGE

A. POULIN, JR. NEW POETS OF AMERICA SERIES, NO. 47

BOA EDITIONS, LTD. ❖ ROCHESTER, NY ❖ 2022

First Edition
22 23 24 25 7 6 5 4 3 2 1

For information about permission to reuse any material from this book, please contact The Permissions Company at www.permissionscompany.com or e-mail permdude@gmail.com.

Publications by BOA Editions, Ltd.—a not-for-profit corporation under section 501 (c) (3) of the United States Internal Revenue Code—are made possible with funds from a variety of sources, including public funds from the Literature Program of the National Endowment for the Arts; the New York State Council on the Arts, a state agency; and the County of Monroe, NY. Private funding sources include the Max and Marian Farash Charitable Foundation; the Mary S. Mulligan Charitable Trust; the Rochester Area Community Foundation; the Ames-Amzalak Memorial Trust in memory of Henry Ames, Semon Amzalak, and Dan Amzalak; the LGBT Fund of Greater Rochester; and contributions from many individuals nationwide. See Colophon on page 74 for special individual acknowledgments.

Cover Design: Sandy Knight
Cover Art: "Shotgun Boogie" by Evita Tezeno
Interior Design and Composition: Richard Foerster
BOA Logo: Mirko

BOA Editions books are available electronically through BookShare, an online distributor offering Large-Print, Braille, Multimedia Audio Book, and Dyslexic formats, as well as through e-readers that feature text to speech capabilities.

Library of Congress Cataloging-in-Publication Data

Names: White, Renia, 1991– author.
Title: Casual conversation / poems by Renia White ; foreword by Aracelis Girmay,
  Blessing the Boats Selection editor-at-large.
Description: First edition. | Rochester, NY : BOA Editions, Ltd., [2022] | Series: A. Poulin, Jr.
  new poets of America series ; no. 47 | Summary: "Renia White's debut poetry collection
  pushes against state-sanctioned authority and societal thought while ruminating on Black joy"
  —Provided by publisher.
Identifiers: LCCN 2021042016 (print) | LCCN 2021042017 (ebook) | ISBN
  9781950774555 (paperback) | ISBN 9781950774562 (ebook)
Subjects: LCGFT: Poetry.
Classification: LCC PS3623.H578748 C37 2022 (print) | LCC PS3623.H578748
  (ebook) | DDC 811/.6—dc23
LC record available at https://lccn.loc.gov/2021042016
LC ebook record available at https://lccn.loc.gov/2021042017

BOA Editions, Ltd.
250 North Goodman Street, Suite 306
Rochester, NY 14607
www.boaeditions.org
A. Poulin, Jr., Founder (1938–1996)

". . . *What we've been trying to figure out how to get to is how we are when we get together to try to figure it out.*"

—Fred Moten

Contents

III.

❖

Foreword

Casual Conversation. I could not get it out of my mind. My mind followed it—Out. It pulled me to the edges of lines into eternities, cessations of sound, simultaneities made emphatic by the enjambment. I began to visit the book as though a place, a friend. I could begin to sense its many saturations and registers of speech, its many ways of listening.

Its gorgeous, subtle strangeness compelled me to read it this way, then that way, reorienting myself to its multiplicities. Here, a spaciousness of phrase gives way to compression. There, the syntax is dense then feathery, as switchgrass. Renia White shimmers a scene and shows us how to listen for the polytemporal dimensions of who and what and how. So much style and meaning and talk and saying hard, true things with such precision that the accounts seem surreal:

> so I walked to the wrong town and built
> a house.   'cause I couldn't confess
> I'd gone the wrong way   confidently.
> due to love, unable to turn around and fail
> in front of everyone   yes, I walked
> to the wrong place   and stayed.

With idiosyncratic brilliance, White offers up an investigative reading of her lives. The result is a formidable, taut, lushtender, mysterious print. In other poems are White's explicit responses to the everyday and ongoing devastations of modernity. White traces the state's shape—those relational and aesthetic configurations that depend on our indoctrinations and subjugations. But her poems are beholden to life, vulnerable to kinship. They cultivate a flourishing grown out of recognition and lucid, effortful attention to one's own becoming. A green grows in the effort, making its way into new and seeking shape, as we see in this excerpt from "the man beside me considers me beside him." She writes:

> . . . the audacity of it, to make
> a world and break it up in small, crafted

planets, small peace amid previously-made terror.
make something grow between fortresses, and badly,

if you are me at least, saying *here something begins
and ends,* but only here. as if you could crop the world

out like an extra head in the frame, own a thing
by seeing it all in one look, make a law by writing

it down or saying it without stammer.

Looking right at us, in poems like this one, White indicts authority and the conditions by which it is created. She cracks the sentences across the jags, yet the lines float with something lyric, fleeting and unowned as breath whirring inside them. Over and over so casually she lays bare the absurdity of carceral, capitalist, and imperialist projects. Again: "as if you could crop the world // out like an extra head in the frame, own a thing / by seeing it all in one look, make a law by writing // it down or saying it without stammer." Her lyric stretches language into something brilliantly resistant to summary and direction, something beautiful and ceaseless as "my mind picks up where I was left," and "we know that you can't slice a chorus into some." There is that chorus again, her mind on the complex, teeming plural.

In *Casual Conversation* White attends to an axiomatic ground in the pagefield. She teaches me something about the collaborative dreaming that we can be. I am saying that there is something for us here in the complex Quiets of this meditative, sustained, and intimately political work. It is something so vital and so unstoppably generative that I can only think to call it unrest.

—aracelis girmay
Brooklyn, NY
2021

hearsay

OK so you are telling me the girl dared say
"I can't just let you have my life,
not like that, your honor"

and he sentenced her to a bedazzled tightrope
and a room without a window, and a son
that doesn't know her name?   middle passage
for this? think the girl doesn't know her own
shame? given that face she wears? think she doesn't
know where she is ain't where she was put down
to begin with?   that her first season was
someone else's harvest?

some people get to want and need
and be met in it.   some just the mouth
just the teeth

some eat and they say
"why all the hunger?"

as far as you know, nothing can kill you

I tumble out my own side window sometimes
it's all the leaning and looking—the hoping
to notice a game-changing glory

my friend likes to say, as long as he is here,
I will not fall all the way down

but let something in me leap off its own mantel
and I am all eyes cast upward and beyond,
wailing   *how?*   and   *despair*

and   *all the women,*
        all the sunless women

yet, every sky I've needed for its beauty has surrendered.
the clouds do go there: the snow and streamers,
the gilded du-rag atop my head

I better not worry nor hang lest
atrocity, atrocity

but people
can only save you
if the timing's right

the man beside me considers me beside him.

1.

I feel it—the human penchant to center oneself.

he is wrong. the him beside me isn't the same man
he experiences himself as. this him is mine

and I say proximity begins here with me.

you too. I have a you of you unseen. it's the only one
I know or believe, ignorant in its precision,

yet made—done. isn't it grotesque? our power?
the axis we can't feel ourselves hanging upon?

2.

once, in a study, asked to pick my own silhouette
from 5 unmarked frames, slightly different each time,

I chose the two largest for safety, and also,
living from a body does make it seem bigger.

looking back, it was comical; I *was* in the middle
right where too much ease would place me. not big,

not small, not mine—a shape without the brain

too tactile, but less a lie when unaffiliated

3.

we take to gardens. the audacity of it, to make
a world and break it up in small, crafted

planets, small peace amid previously-made terror.
make something grow between fortresses, and badly,

if you are me at least, saying *here something begins
and ends*, but only here. as if you could crop the world

out like an extra head in the frame, own a thing
by seeing it all in one look, make a law by writing

it down or saying it without stammer.

my mother wants to live in a gated community

I am only crying because she might want to infer that she's worth defense.
the fact will be embedded, you see?   she is thinking about something
akin to value   and the metric is another latch on another outside.
the metric is insisting upon an out   that need stay there.

the thing about an unmanned gate is, something can walk right in.   then what?
it's there—inside.   equivalent   crossed over the flimsy membrane of
don't come any further   simply because you didn't make it less possible.

+

I once tried to stop something in its tracks because the saying says so, right?
and so I stood there, in the way of something   and there I was, ran over
'cause the advancing thing was stronger in a superficial way.
just the figure.   so, the politic. the jacket. all skin.

the way they made it seem in shows, I figured there'd be more
moats and quicksand.   I figured we had a door
because there was something   out there.

in this village

in this village we measure the distance between
the prayer and its mouth, the chorus and each of its pains.

we know that you can't slice a chorus into some,
that if you separate the mouth from what it yells,

the yell is just an announcement in the spirit of itself.
the kids know well enough to say, *why I gotta die to be*

a body? but then the elders say, *I even died in the spirit of being alive.*
to which the kids reply, *I am not here in the spirit of myself*

or something dead. I came in the thing I pray with and for.
and some of the elders cry while playing the same old song

anew. say *finally.* and *at last.*
and *in the beginning*

casual conversation

when a girl falls to her knees in the woods
she could be kneeling for prayer even
when it seems she couldn't

believing in possibility is like that:
a way to hide from what
history has told us

listen,

they just found a man hanging from a tree in

my God
                                Mississippi
        oh Lord

this could also be his way of choosing.

thank God for the possibility
of a choosing ghost. thank God
the mothers still know

their sons into remembering: that
each neck's story still has three sides.

thank our spent God who knows the rope
and hand, the diameter of a kneeling knee,
how it came to kneel,

what will stab at the thin skin, that it will be less
than whatever left a man hovering above ground.

thank our prickling God
            and his tongue

waiting to meet us with our answer,
            our ghosts

that trouble

I am not prepared for the inverse of this.

if everything always brings with it its opposite,
every time something happens, one can ask
"what if it hadn't?"   and still be relevant

how dangerous a logic we've made

proof is what happens afterward, to show us
the during was true. we had to find a way
to promise what we are doing is worthwhile

so we decided to imprint the now
for later, after

perhaps we cannot be trusted to remember.
perhaps we know that a new dream is a correction
of the old one, no matter what we mean to feel.

so you walk the street two minutes too late,
and so you live, or miss your old lover, or your new one,
or   in pursuit of ourselves, we can meet another us
and so on.

        then, one day, a sad woman enters you and clears
        your desk.   says, "I am the new"

and what do you say to such a gentle intrusion?
so sure of itself?

you'll think someone else organized it.
you'll think it must be yours.

all over, but only here

girl in a town up to its wrists in water
girl in a town inventing a fix for the drowning

it's called leaving

in a town that runs from itself—girl coming upon woman
and water   come upon yourself.

the man pays you a visit.

it is all self-serving. you need the leaving to meet you.
he grabs your wrist and admires the slim of it, the soft.

says, "it feels like this
          all over, doesn't it?"

he means the soft. you swerve and miss the actual.
pretend he means the drowning. so yea. *yea.*

all over, but only here.

he thinks you are made of something he needs so he smiles
though he doesn't feel it. you don't love him at all, really

just the elsewhere he brings you.

you touch sometimes, pretend you are sorry and without footing.
he doesn't even feel it for what it is.

you think: we could drown and we wouldn't even fill.

you can give a body what it says it wants and if it doesn't know
that's what it's getting it can refuse to sink or float

can refuse to receive. can hang its mouth waiting to drink
when it's already drowning

in this town

there is a girl soundless as a good bulb.
so quiet, there is nothing to report

one day she saw something, and after that
everyone could see it on her although
it wasn't there—that kind of girl.

somewhere else, a pair, though uncoupling,
eats dinner at a table the shape of
a seashell.

some things are real ornate here
heavy at the bottom.

there is a house of unloved things
in which the plant, the table runner,
the gilded mirror all say
"that ain't what we call this place"

and, by the way, at that couple's dinner
beginning the end of all soft, the woman asked
her lover: *when I die, will you speak at my funeral?*
say I was good?

> *depends on when you die,* he said

she would have unfastened herself to know
but, luckily, at that hour, a church congregation
had been praying the wind westward

in this town, where preachers practice their sermons
in garages for the acoustics, all the signs mean what
they say, and when something burns down, it isn't

all together again in the next scene

when you look as if you'll speak, a dying woman turns to you
and adds: *before you ask—yes, I did send my references.*
before I even entered the room, in went strangers
promising that I would be good

a different, younger woman overhears and complains
that no one ever asks her any of the questions her life
has answered   and yet: yes, the door is golden
on both sides yes, it is easier to break

what you barely touch   no, there is nothing
you can do

cue the lights

mother's on enough medication to heal something, I hope.

meanwhile, Black women vote for who we must, for the God-flock's

better wind.　　　　　the same week Kim Porter died, I briefly lost my vision

on a Broad St. bound J.　　　my head buzzed in pain; I was a circuit for worry

to get home through.　but this city ain't my home. this frame ain't the same one

I always had, ain't the same one I see in the God-mirror.　　sometimes I think:

please don't let me almost die　　　　because it will happen quicker—

once it's over our fence it just dies easier.　　don't ask me how.

all the numbers say it.　　and my body dare touch a brink?

on a crowded train? in a city that ain't mine? while I'm off

the shore of myself?　and she left behind all that joy?

you know how many on their way to joy, and then

down the center of it all—a bright unknown?

then the flowers?　　the refrain?

misgiving

I followed you down the road of yourself,
and when we found the uglies, you said
     don't look   and I said, *but*
I am here, in you.

you brought me here to show me
what not to look at.   I misheard
what you called this and yourself,
but I knew not to guess aloud, not to grasp
anything by what it incited.   in order to
love you, I had to forget my first thought.

so I walked to the wrong town and built
a house.   'cause I couldn't confess
I'd gone the wrong way   confidently.
due to love, unable to turn around and fail
in front of everyone   yes, I walked
to the wrong place   and stayed.

some plans should be thwarted

I announce within myself *I wanna live real quick*
and it's revealed—the way to tilt toward unending.

I come back into the moment I never left   with my bleaker
self clutched against my chest   and I have never danced so

right after an unraveling?   looking at a morning
finding glim where filth once glinted?   touching

the hem of the star inside us all?

36c

the first time a boy asked me about my breasts
we were on the front steps of Abyssinia Baptist
and those boys everybody knew weren't saved,
just brothers, had rode in with us
on the vacation bible school van
with that door you had to dislocate
your shoulder just to close.
and I can't say I wasn't intrigued
but something about the moment felt like
maybe girl, go prove you talk to God
like you know him. so I tattled
and my church uncle grabbed that boy,
just a brother, up by his ear with a twist
so hard I heard it pop like a knuckle.
and if I knew then those brothers
would remain as unsaved as before,
that no vestibule assault would
take his eyes off my sprouting,
that just 'cause you've got a ticket
doesn't mean you'll get in,
I would've told him, *36C like grown women*
like I wanted, like it was some shame to know
all by myself so I had to let him in.
and maybe he'd have saved me,
that boy, just a brother, all Black and real
solid, real wiry, in on the joke so soon
he couldn't help himself

half dozens

you so unkempt
nothing want you but the vultures

you been stood up so much
you sunflower,

you marching band,
all brass and not even marching. you

a band that don't move   just try, just muster and fail,
sounding like a stampede of shiny buckles
that don't work.

you extra letter in a misspelled word,
looking at you make my eyes itch, looking like an inside voice's
redaction.   you so vase with cracks you can't catch your own seep.

you unspeakable—don't know whether you spacesuit
or gurney. half-steeped "this'll make you feel better" tea
drinking, ain't got a boy to your name

mountain of monstrosity.

ol' blindfold and spin
yourself then tell somebody you're lost,
need a boost from the world,

ol' thought you loved a man
'cause you felt him under your skin like a sound
but forgot to listen for its borders, you all sensation,
miss everything that ever happened to everybody

but you, you wallow and silkworm, crusted over
from all that remembering, your ol'

so behind
time is waiting on you to get on with this
self

just gorgeous

november 9, 2016

they hate themselves so much they prove it.   look at everyone   not looking at
me. don't.   don't look at my body or through it. I need less "seen" anyway—its
streamered flesh,   its daunt and sparkle.   at the end of every book
there is a way to re-enter, to enter the next, or a door so heavy   you know it will
shut with a tremor.   I have read this one before, but it always begs me to
choose   my own adventure   of a life.
so dark and stratified,   you'd think it a country   that is hard to look
away from.   I am trying to say, I look as if I am not of this place   to that
point where you know I am.   I wonder how it feels   to have a want you aren't
surrendering
'cause you always had it   like a right.   I wonder what it's like to have a right and
believe it so much, you act in it without fear.   congratulations,
you have chosen what makes it easier to not see me with difficulty.   I understand
how hard it can be to know   in order for you to eat, someone else had to starve.
in order for you to see, someone else had to be   the thing you're not   staring at.

in the name of half-sistering

while she slept, I searched her half-dead for its secret,
special percentage. perhaps the nose. I never quite felt
connected to her nose—the way she ate salt from her palm
then scrunched it perfect.

this is the part where an all-knowing enters, says
and that is how you break a two   or

where is your father in you?

trust me, we asked ourselves.
in our shared room, before our shared mirror,
we looked for our other families.

8 and 9, respectively, told that we belong
to someone else by the girl with rough knees
and a slug tongue who stole my turn in double-dutch
and my sister wasn't having it.

slug tongue said,   *she just your half-sister*
                          y'all ain't got the same daddy

asphalt and sliver us
why don't you?

build a wedge called daddy and gulf us
in the name of your stolen thing.

a sister ain't a partial feeling. she so mine, we so sistered,
each of us asked the other if we should confirm with ma
then *knew*

both of us, together

knew

that wasn't even our question.

the space between

the story lost itself, but you were afraid and I know it. I know when you are the things you are because you were once my big sister, once told me I could catch the sun in a Ziploc bag and I knew you were lying then but I jumped, jumped just to amuse you because I felt something in you needed me to believe.   and that night I speak of was real fear for you   me too.   I was in the car of my then boyfriend. he and I were kissing in his bug parked next to a cop car
we didn't notice 'til your body went slam against its hood and how you cried NO, no, no, NO, I didn't do anything, swear   how you swore NO, tussled with that officer saying *please*.   how could we know that fear   is nothing but power going in the wrong direction?
so I couldn't speak, just cried without the tears   if God resides in every country why he don't show his face right now? rip my sister from this devil thing?   and that officer just held you—smirking, her grip 'round your chain.   Lord, if you are the after and the law precedes,   I know the hands before did not wash clean, the hands before do not meet for grace   and why must I learn this way   which hands can't unhinge what doctrine made?   must accept.   must yearn for the pop of your latch lying "free" like someone else said it   'cause someone else said it

to banish

a hole in a window is a hole in a hole already functioning
a hole in a mother is a daughter in a twin bed and another
out too late, banished again   wherever she is
beyond the back bedroom and its blister of carpet

beneath the venetian-blinded window,
a daughter in a twin bed awaiting the return

a hole in a sister is a hole in a wall   is a window
a way to enter what hurt you where it hurt you

a mother and daughter argue about a boy who would
unhinge his wrist against a sister told not to return
if she chooses to leave again, out late again
to let the puckers settle

a hole is a window is a hole in a house   can let in
things unwanted   the way thinking yourself unwanted
can bring you to a window   with its own tapping
plea and whisper

a sister—out of bed   pulls, with elbow crease under pit,
her sister   through the gap   sure to clasp the open
with a sound meant for hearing by her mother, next door,
never quite sleeping   until she hears the close again

you could have come in through the front door

beneath

when I say love is an undertaking, I don't mean
the man speaks so highly of the woman
it's as if she's dead.

I am not invoking the feeling of having a body
that requires tending. I do not mean the expense

and will not argue with the man who tells me
poetry is like life insurance.   but if it were, the way
desiring protection can leave one imagining dying

based off seeing it happen to someone else, based off
the probability that it will certainly happen to everyone

even the man you love,
I am saying, I don't need to see the entrails to know;
we are wired to make it stop or happen neater

                              +

one evening—in an effort to keep him living—a couple,
though uncommitted, put all their hands beneath a guy
choking on his own vomit, to turn him toward the light,

I figured, to spare him such an unloving end: the last
train car, none of the stillness dying merits.

from my seat, I watched and thought   *God,   we are being outlived
somewhere, always.*   that death is time successfully closing
fingers 'round a wrist.   that love is choosing to make it fail

casual conversation

I wanna see less

        when I look at a life

but all the buttons and bullets

        riddling everything.

the way we can say

        and all the gilding everywhere

and go *mmhmm*

        mmhmm.

my lover's mouth is gilded

        with my name.

my dream mouth gilded

        with rose gold fronts

my childhood stippled

        with what we put away

where we put it and why

        gilds our town of

Manifest, Manifest.

          my favorite boy shining

my sister out of jail

          my mind picks up where I was left

conjuring
(14850)

in this part, a window is the membrane
between inheritance and the inner

by 'inner' I mean, if you look on the middle shelf
of your understanding, you will always find something
you didn't put there, but could have

so you move to a town you've never heard of
telling everyone *I wouldn't have come if I'd known*
and the home you choose lets a bat through the window
because you called it to yourself

all the holes
all the creaking
all the sunflowers ornate 'til they die

you think a bat is here because a window is?
everything you've met was coming for you
ask yourself what it satisfies   let's start there

challenger

1.
no one notices it tastes like nothing but heat.
we are kings of it, us darker folks, so I notice,
but this isn't about me.   let's be honest:
you'd expect more from me at a hot sauce party.

and perhaps you can't take everything inside
with you everywhere; no outside food in the theater,
no backward hymn in the church. but if a man can
unload a gun in both, if that can be necessary,

let me tell you about how I took to the hot sauce
expo the feeling that, perhaps, your hot sauce
tastes a lot like nothing.   ask me the intricacies
of heat and sweet, maybe even savory. I can take
you there, where they shake apart.

2.
the crowd barks as an unfazed woman eats
seventeen peppers without requesting her glass
of milk. they repeat that these are hot enough
to burn eyes. this must be torture. she is
superhuman. (did I mention Black also?)

3.
taken by an urge unnecessary for the cause,
my mind doesn't wanna cheer her on. she'll win
a title, they say. she's a finalist, and so close, and so
unmoved.   I think she looks a little like my mama.
I think she's better than your pepper trophy.

4.
I think of useful heat—the kind some use to light
incense, dead things for eating, wads of hair
for luck, churches for hate, people, more specific
people—highly specific in tint and accusation.

5.
I didn't mean to bring anything extra in, but
where is the mind capable of un-taking me?
maybe I do want her to win. maybe
she'll grab the mike and blow flames.
make us cinder.

6.
in the final round, her opponent is revealed:
white man, adequate belly, curly hair, family present,
fully expecting a victory. and she tried and so did he
—20 something odd peppers, I believe. you must
chew. you must swallow after chewing.
open your mouth to prove it.

and of course, of course he won.
it was close, but his family looked unmoved, entirely.
I mean, he was the reigning champ; the woman,
just a challenger.   of course, of course.

lump

              in this part the girl is without head.
         I draw her bone-jut and sweet—
an extravagant lump referencing what isn't present.

it's been said before that if I don't
say a thing, but imply it, you will think it.

perhaps a headless girl can be imagined humanely.
          perhaps this girl will be treated as if she were
              headed. draw her formless as if to say

imagine form here.
gonna make me a girl

you can't arm sling and knee press. gonna make me
         a girl with all her broken showing 'top the skin,
            a siren of infant wails to prove her girlhood.

gonna color her in with what
it takes to make a girl just a girl,

           perhaps not the crime it is to be too specific
       other.   gonna make me a girl you can't knee press,
officer. make her of ground she's already down on.

you can't tell her "get down" further if she is
ground itself. gonna make her the kind of nothing

you can still imagine as your daughter. not too dark,
         not so un-girled by her something-ness
            that she can't be nothing enough

for you
to be soft with.

love can make a man forget

1.

run your eyes along the boy
as you'd pink salt rim a glass
soon as he says he will make
the drive tonight

two nights after they killed
that other boy who don't
look much like your boy
except the

. . . you know . . .

skin then spoon-batter a soft
egg. yolk, sturdy kiss, butter him
into better thinking. and if he
still don't get it, touch

like potential dead
'til there's nothing to do
but love-make.

2.

begin and end with these body machines
sensing the death towns over
like a knee does rain.

girl says, that happens to women too

about a thing a Black woman says
happened to her, possibly,
don't know unless someone other
than her saw, of course.

I forgive her though she will never seek it

though she will never seek woman in me

will never see me and say
woman.

I attempt to draw a line down myself
where my being Black and woman
begin, end, spiral

sever the spin from the top
deciding just to hear the whir

everything about her is everything about me
until only one of us can be halved at once
and then

girl, you know you know

let the choir sing

meanwhile

the girl at the end of the road you aren't taking is still there.

she has heft to her, declaratively.

it's uncomfortable, I know, to think of the things you break
as broken by you.

why must they insist upon their truths like that?

scream it and get it behind you already:

some men could kill a man.   some men look at me
and think,
        let's make a world minus this—

it's true. walk about the room softly,
touch nothing on your way out.

/Black girl\ something about your existence
proves they can't say it didn't happen because
how else did you get here?

                    meanwhile,

a girl throws herself down the fickle steps of a man's desire
and doesn't come back up until someone goes to get her

     and accumulating

sometimes I flash forward and cry

I am afraid to have this thought.

a 1.5 bedroom apartment in a city I can bear,

metallic hangers and art featuring dark girls,
their faces obscured by large flowers
and overgrown fruit

a bed so heavy it startles the sinking hips

a man with my feet in his hands
who half-coos, "I bet you were hard
to find before I found you"

all the things glimmering,

the man's eyes growling,

each fruit unripe

everything wishing
to be unfound

aurify

in her town, A buries a yellow bird
refers to it as *a gesture of care*
because she can see the world
in the small   knows that a bird is
a speck of the God-flock

I lean in because I need to—
for the sake of staying around
in the name of the sun inside us all

droned to her about my makings
and then she tells me this? I can't help
myself. I needed the dead wonder.
needed someone to know I too have
my ear to the root. it is between us now
—the yellow bird that gilts us

making your way

there. push through the man's sleeping chest. you've got it. you are just as ghost as you believe. imagine your loved one come to you and say 'I am ghost' and you love them so much they've reached that space where they can't be wrong or zany, just themselves being. imagine your lover saying 'I am ghost' and pushing hard on the wall and then saying she's through and with satisfaction. what if she also says something completely true and germy like: people can do without you. they have and they will. before they met you they were without you and while you are with them you are not always, unless you are ghost. I am ghost and now I'm always where I say I am because I say it and perhaps this is enough to convince you to push through your lover's chest. you will rouse him, sure. and he will ask what you are doing. be honest. say, "I am trying to get to the pit inside you where I lost something valuable." say you are ghost and you are making your way in, in. say this and by the response you will know how thorough the love. it is thin, of course, if he goes toward his own belief and need. it is thin if he questions what else makes you ghost beyond the declaration. thin if he says you were not ghost yesterday or when he met you. everyone knows that what you are changes no matter how still you sit. if he calls a bigger name to come and take you, it is thin. he don't believe in you with enough risk and unearthliness. make joke of it and leave him in the morning.

but it is thick if he surrenders, follows, amends. says, how deep you trynna go? can I help? I felt you there already, I think, if you thought I did, if you wanted me to. I'll will the feeling. make it up like everything else we make up which is everything. time. fire. words for things they say we don't quite make up the yearning for like "need" or "love." then you know he has the space-making ability to usher in a new love: a sense of yearning to be taken and done something with. and he's lying like the rest and maybe the surrender ain't real, but listen to what I say and make it the thing you need it to be. push through your sleeping lover's chest and there will always be an in. go.

to hover

consider my hand on the crack in your wood-stained shelf—the crack you haven't
caused yet—and still, my hand hovers over where the machine of it buzzes
each finger a potential splinter

I miss the crack the way you can miss a thing you haven't had, simply because
it's been had before across some border, inside some boudoir.   the way a hand
knows wound to come when it feels it coming on

you don't know what's in you and I don't either, but look at what we do have:
dark skin—both of us—big teeth, a pair of eyes, each
a something we saw happen.

I know you thought you threw it away and it crawled back down your sleeping
throat   and you're gonna break this shelf somehow   drop
something heavy on it, let time undo it,   make it buckle

under some brand of pressure   and me too
and I to you, my not-yet love   at rest, which invokes its own rising
or that thing I see floating above your face

un–

I don't mean to bring it back here:
the carpet sore beneath the undone window,
the small opening making open the big thing,
the etcetera, etcetera, dead folks, etcetera,

but I need to know what undoes itself?
what kind of latch without hand?

this is our undoing. woman beside me in the café
says this massacre is so like us. I think of the "us"
this takes   then,
she might not mean "our" us, maybe *their* us.

but maybe we got an us too: me, her,
everyone who decides to have it.

I think that's what she's hoping for—distance,
something to climb out of herself through.

you know how you can undo a whole home
with the unlatching of a window? howl from the pit
beneath it? say "we did this" and "we allowed this"

and the girl beside you will forget you are white, maybe
will not query your us-ing. will not ask which "us"

of this country

will not actually say *Charleston.*

will leave you a window, open.

"Bree climbed that flagpole with such grace,"
she says. undid the flag. the window is open still.
left it open, kept the flag, let out no howl

the opposite of howling, actually
this is the perfect time to sing

we, we, we, we

yet and still the churches burn, the window's open,
closing it will not save us, another window won't save us.

who is us and what are we and what do you do
with an open thing

that can't be fixed by closing?

I know you don't need me

we are far beyond need.
all of us—wanted
tethered to some kind of want,
wretched or not.

there are too many of us
to explain otherwise.
someone wanted this reality
to be possible for me.

someone wanted me into existence.
and I know you don't need me,
but when I was born, a song began
to play   and I like it.   it is playing
for my liking, exclusively.

if you touch me, you'll have touched
a someone: rightly loved and lived for.

now, on purpose, I have requested
something small that you owe me.
give it here because it's owed
not because I asked.   I never did ask,
but told you   I am here and I wanna be

plush

a dark, lush stole 'round the neck of a woman
whose gait says   *see me when you see me*

I mean, really look.   or one day a tree fell
and announced itself.   became
your kind of loud.

ambit

it wasn't mine to begin with
the want I began thinking toward
pushing my life in the wagon of

        in the mistake room

when a thing that was never
going to happen doesn't
we will think there is no more gold
and so there will be no more gold

until we forget its taste
by grazing something else
become a new strain
of ourselves

why everybody wanna be singular?

I insist upon the chorus of myself.
a lover I never had stands at his kitchen counter
hiding behind the last clean glass, head bowed, crying
because I'm away or not his yet.   or he is looking for me
in a mug or upturned palm the way a woman in a tarot shop
(that is really her living room) would.   that happened once
and it was doing the telling.   the man and I shouldn't have been.
I didn't realize, even when she didn't bother to read our fortunes
differently. all our palms in the same room, she stared at the floor
and said, "you want to be good; you want people to think you are good"

+

he is and I am and we are as now as sometimes
I weep shower apologies for men I tried to throw myself
away from who came back from the almost-left to tell me
girl, I suppose I could   but, I'm tired

+

mole on the lip of one, scar at the brow of another—
reduced to the markings, men are larger narratives
with a single, lingering detail
some other force inscribed

+

one walks into the front of my temple, bird-smash into the door
before knocking.   it looks like everything he's ever gone through,
every permeable, feminine everlasting.   I am watching from
the tower, hoping he makes it all the way up here   so I know
it can be done.   I believe, but I'd like to know too.

surplus

the men chase me very much unlike a butterfly,
possibly a storm. look at this happening to me,
they say, you are the kind of woman that *happens*.

the production is always dress rehearsing,
never jaw-wide and ready, but pretending to be,
performing as if to perform again as the real thing.

an abandoned school bus is real, but it's got so much extra.
so much surplus. all those seats, the tooth-clanging
yellow of it, the abandonment itself: just a thing
someone came to, just a thing a person did.

we chase storms and marvel at the stranded, but
those are just things that happened, really, if you say.
I am just a woman happening to a man, so I talk
from my feet, dangle my strange-perfect.

now the sad gal is giving a lesson on joy-making,
walking a putrid, pink bridge   and the man's so done,
but he wants to be where the ache takes place.
makes soft where it isn't. smiles. joy-*makes*.

all these feelings between us do nothing more than
glitch us   make us further incomprehensible.
all the things you say just leave you, you know?
nothing for them to stick to but a man maybe.
how unreliable. and so *much* to it.

gather them & give them back to me.

(after Toni Morrison)

I don't have the wherewithal to die today,
not with you here. (thank you for that)
you say things could be simple, and sometimes
they are. it's true, we only need what we need
in order to have all we need. nothing more,
but love, which is a texture you say you don't
understand. but look at this bread in my mouth
and your hand in mine although we barely touch
because how outlandish—to feel even further? beyond
the sure blessing? so your hand isn't in mine, but I feel
it there—when I am asleep, awake, inside my mind room.
I touch everything I walk by or into. but, you   here?
and us with hands in case we need them?   I think this is it,
but if you want to make it more complicated, I agree.

in case you'd consider it

a vacation is a personal decision
a sign you hang in your own script

I am a woman made of flesh (first in this
context) and, somehow, the cashier asked
the second woman in line for her order

I have never understood my look
and how others understand it

I have things I wanna hide from, but
for every bridge I've built above, I've jumped
back below   into my own blue rummage

I've never kept anything I feared I wouldn't,
my anxieties have been proven, and perhaps
the knuckle and gash of the world
are true as a timeclock is true

but I am on vacation from that ache
on vacation from the way it looks and what
it brings.   don't have to answer to it

because I declared *not now.*
and some things are respected, once claimed

some things get what they're due

bright, bright, bright

I ask the hue to smatter me lovely in your name
yellow-bloused barista
Black girl with careful hands—all you did
was wear a color   and here I am
wishing all the lights aglow in your hope room

Notes

The epigraph comes from an audio conversation between Fred Moten and Stefano Harvey for the Poetry Project, April 24, 2015.

Kim Porter was a model and actress. ("cue the lights")

Bree Newsome is an artist and activist who, in 2015, climbed the flagpole in front of the South Carolina Capitol building, lowering the confederate battle flag. ("un-")

From Toni Morrison's *Beloved*: "She is a friend of my mind. She gather me, man. The pieces I am, she gather them and give them back to me in all the right order." ("gather them & give them back to me.")

Acknowledgments

Thank you to the editorial teams of the following publications in which the listed poems previously appeared:

No, Dear: "all over, but only here";
Poetry Daily: "un-" (reprint);
Prelude: "girl says, that happens to women too," "half dozens," "making your way," "un-";
Puerto del Sol: "aurify";
Ruminate Magazine: "in this village";
Slice: "the man beside me considers me beside him.";
Sonora Review: "casual conversation," "in the name of half-sistering," "the space between"
Southern Indiana Review: "hearsay";
Stone Canoe: "sometimes I flash forward and cry";
The New Guard: "36C";
The Southampton Review: "in this town," "my mother wants to live in a gated community," "to hover";
The Offing: "love can make a man forget";
Witness: "lump."

I'm thankful, also, for the programs and facilitators that helped shape my work as I thought toward this book. My gratitude to Howard University and Tony Medina, especially, for the space where I first considered doing this tinkering, where I first saw the possibility.

My thanks to Cornell's MFA program for the time to dedicate myself to the work of poetry. For everything, everything, I thank Lyrae Van Clief-Stefanon (a gift, a dream) and Ishion Hutchinson. Their grace and insight helped illuminate the path for this collection.

Many of these poems benefited from the conversations and questions of my cohort and beyond. My thanks to Aricka Foreman, Richard LaRose, Aurora

Masum-Javed, Korey Williams, Liza Flum, Emily Oliver, Harper Quinn, Evelynn Yuen, Samson Jardine, and Mandy Gutmann-Gonzalez. For their guidance, I thank Dagmawi Woubshet and Valzyhna Mort. For friendship and support that has helped sustain me in this practice, I thank Lanre Akinsiku.

The community and/or resources of the BOAAT Retreat, Sonora Review, and the Hurston/Wright Foundation: I am so grateful for their offerings. I thank Eduardo C. Corral for his teachings and affirmations.

I am indebted to the gift of Aracelis Girmay—for her immaculate eye and all that she has given this landscape. I'm grateful to BOA Editions for bringing this work to the world.

My deepest gratitude to my friends and family who show me that it's OK to reach toward them in our daily lives and in these poems. I'm thankful for all your listening and thinking through; you light my life from within. Korede Bandele-Thomas, heart of all hearts, thank you.

Shelly and Frances, my mother and grandmother, thank you for your gems, your wit, and your pressing on. Caleb, Kiera, and Shayla: I am forever dreaming and thinking alongside you.

About the Author

Renia White is a writer originally from Maryland. After coming of age in Riverdale, Georgia, she earned her BA from Howard University and her MFA from Cornell University. A recipient of the 2015 Hurston/Wright College Writers Award in poetry and the 2016 Sonora Review Poetry Prize, in 2021, she also received the Philip Freund Prize for Creative Writing. She lives and teaches in New York City.

BOA Editions, Ltd.
The A. Poulin, Jr. New Poets of America Series

Colophon

Blessing the Boats Selection titles spotlight poetry collections by women of color. The series is named in honor of Lucille Clifton (1936–2010) whose poetry collection *Blessing the Boats: New and Selected Poems 1988–2000* (BOA Editions) received the National Book Award. In 1988, Lucille Clifton became the first author to have two collections selected in the same year as finalists for the Pulitzer Prize: *Good Woman: Poems and a Memoir 1969–1980* (BOA), and *Next: New Poems* (BOA). Among her many other awards and accolades are the Ruth Lilly Poetry Prize, the Frost Medal, and an Emmy Award. In 2013, her posthumously published collection *The Collected Poems of Lucille Clifton 1965–2010* (BOA) was awarded the Hurston/Wright Legacy Award for Poetry.

The publication of this book is made possible, in part,
by the support of the following patrons:

Lannan Foundation
Anonymous
Bernadette Catalana
Anne Coon & Craig Zicari
Christopher C. Dahl, *in memory of J. D. McClatchy*
Joseph Finetti & Maria Mastrosimone
Alison Granucci
James Long Hale
Margaret Heminway
Sandi Henschel
Nora A. Jones
Paul LaFerriere & Dorrie Parini
John & Barbara Lovenheim
Joe McElveney
Boo Poulin
Deborah Ronnen
William Waddell & Linda Rubel